M000313678

RICK RODGERS

BRIDAL AND BABY SHOWERS

Surefire recipes and exciting menus for a flawless party!

ILLUSTRATIONS BY ROBBIN GOURLEY

WARNER TREASURES™

PUBLISHED BY WARNER BOOKS

A TIME WARNER COMPANY

Warner Treasures is a trademark of Warner Books, Inc.

Warner Books, Inc.
1271 Avenue of the Americas
New York, NY 10020

 A Time Warner Company

Book design by Robbin Gourley
Printed in Singapore
First Printing: March 1996
10 9 8 7 6 5 4 3 2 1

ISBN: 0-446-91097-X

CONTENTS

INTRODUCTION

WHILE I AM ALWAYS ready to celebrate good times and good food with my friends and family, there are two occasions that demand extra-special attention: the announcement of a wedding or an upcoming birth. These two events are particularly joyous as they represent such important concepts in our lives as love, family, and the continuation of life. And they are excellent reasons to give a fine party.

A party, yes, but this is an extraordinary party because weddings and births are extraordinary times for the celebrants. It's a party with flair and elegance to distinguish it from the casual parties given throughout the year. It's an affair that calls for fine china and silver, linen napkins, and gorgeous flowers. Here's a chance for the guests to wear their most fashionable outfits and look and feel their best—an occasion for delicious food and beverages.

After years of catering in Manhattan and California, I learned that the secret of a wonderful party is good planning. The food must be beautiful and mouthwatering, yes, but its service must be orchestrated so that the food is served at its best—no soggy sandwiches or unappetizingly tepid dishes! This little book offers tested menus and suggestions (including timetables for advance preparation and other helpful hints) on how to create an elegant bridal shower or a perfect celebration tea for the expectant mother.

A bridal shower often calls for feeding a large crowd a substantial meal, and the invitation list usually is longer than for other kinds of parties. It may be the first time both sides of the family are getting together, and co-workers may also be invited. Rather than just putting out a couple of bowls for nibbles, snacks, and dips, you can set a celebratory tone with a full meal. A buffet is certainly a more efficient way to serve than a sit-down dinner, and the bridal shower buffet menu in this book has been planned for optimum ease, equally appropriate as an early afternoon brunch or lunch or as a supper. All of the dishes are make-ahead, and the main dishes can all be served at room temperature. I have chosen dishes that are easy to make in multiple batches, or even divide, as needed, so you can prepare just as much food as necessary. However, be sure that you have enough refrigerator space, stamina, and seating before you decide to be your own caterer. I recommend a maximum of thirty guests for a nonprofessional to handle in an average-size home.

An afternoon baby shower calls for lighter fare but a tasteful, stylish repast nonetheless. To me, a proper tea fills the bill. A tea party has always been the epitome of high style and class (just ask the Windsors), but it need not be a stuffy affair. While there are traditions to a tea service (cucumber sandwiches and the like), I have had some fun with the menu and offer famil-

iar teatime foods in updated versions. Not everyone is lucky enough to have a family heirloom silver tea service, but the necessary implements are easily acquired from your local party rental service. The sight of a gleaming samovar on a beautifully set table is a glorious one, indeed.

Showers used to be considered as female get-togethers with a fair portion of chitchat and gossip, always off-limits to men. But this is an old-fashioned image and you should not exclude guests on the basis of gender. Just as the workplace has diversified, so too men are now invited to baby and bridal showers. Many showers include the groom and father-to-be, and their friends also, so don't feel that the affair has to be particularly feminine in style. The key word is *elegance:* give a shower that will show your pride in the milestone your friend or relative has reached.

So let's lift our Champagne glasses (or teacups) in a toast to the lucky couple or parents-to-be—and while we're at it, maybe our forks, as well.

A BRIDAL SHOWER BUFFET

Tropical Iced Tea Punch with Fruit Ice Ring
Sparkling Wine

HORS D' OEUVRES
SPICY PARMESAN PALMIERS
CORN AND ROSEMARY MADELEINES

BUFFET
CHICKEN BREASTS STUFFED WITH HERBS AND CHEESE,
WITH SWEET RED PEPPER SAUCE
COUSCOUS SALAD WITH SAFFRON VINAIGRETTE
BEET AND CARROT SALAD WITH WALNUT DRESSING
FRESH BAKED ROLLS*

TORTA DI TIRAMISÙ
YOUR FAVORITE FRESH FRUIT SALAD*
Coffee and Tea

For 12 people

*Recipe not included

A BEAUTIFULLY PREPARED buffet is one of the most satisfying ways to feed a crowd of bridal shower guests. But like any successful party, a buffet takes forethought and planning, beginning with the menu. After creating hundreds of buffets as a caterer, I learned the dos and don'ts that ensure a winning meal.

Most parties begin with hors d'oeuvres served while the guests mingle for beverages. Avoid passed hors d'oeuvres unless you hire a service staff for heating, garnishing, and passing; otherwise, you will find yourself in the kitchen constantly fussing with the appetizers instead of talking with your company. Choose appetizers that can be placed in different areas of the party space and be served at room temperature. Spicy Parmesan Palmiers and Corn and Rosemary Madeleines are both savory versions of favorite French sweets. They are delicious, and they have interesting, conversation-making shapes. Also, they can be prepared weeks ahead of time and frozen, a bonus for the cook.

Try to keep the invitees to a reasonable number, remembering that they all have to find some place to sit and eat. As the food may be eaten off of plates they will hold in their laps, avoid sauces that can drip onto dresses and ties. Choose colorful, full-flavored foods that need a minimum of last-minute attention or garnishing. Dishes served at room temperature work best. Chicken Breasts Stuffed with Herbs and Cheese, with Sweet Red Pepper Sauce meets all these criteria (served with just a dab of a thick sauce that won't threaten silk finery), plus it is a main course that everyone will love.

The menu should feature items that can be prepared well ahead without any deterioration in quality. In fact, some foods are better if made a day or two ahead, such as marinated vegetable salads. The Couscous Salad with Saffron Vinaigrette and the Beet and Carrot Salad with Walnut Dress-

ing are two that always get applause. Lastly, a well-made buffet ends with a spectacular dessert. One of the most popular desserts today is *tiramisù,* which I have transformed into Torta di Tiramisù, a layer cake frosted with rich mascarpone cheese and sprinkled with chocolate shavings.

Little things are always appreciated at a large meal—your guests will be touched by your attention to detail. Here are a few ideas: offer a fresh fruit salad with dessert, not just to complement the cake but to have something for those who may be dieting, and brew a flavored coffee (hazelnut vanilla is a personal favorite). Serve the hot beverages with imported demerara sugar crystals, and place a bowl of fresh unhulled strawberries or a plate of chocolates on the buffet table after the dessert has been served.

Your planning should include the table setting. Draw a "map" of the serving table that includes the platters, flowers, and so on. Take all your tableware and serving platters out of the closet or china cabinet and clean them a few days ahead. (Don't forget to polish any silver, and send out the linen to the cleaners, too.) You may want to stack the plates, napkins, and forks on a cloth-draped sideboard or card table to alleviate crowding at the buffet table. Don't lay the flatware in rows—it takes up too much space. Tie

the forks and napkins in colorful ribbons, then stack them in a basket decorated with a ribbon and a bow. Place the basket at the opposite end of the table, away from the plates, giving the guests one less thing to juggle while they serve themselves. I make two stacks of plates and place them on opposite sides of the table. That way there can be two lines, as guests can serve themselves from both sides. Put two serving utensils in each dish so the line will move even faster. (Everyone hates long buffet lines.)

For an extra-special meal, sparkling wine is the beverage to serve. It doesn't have to be an expensive French Champagne, unless all your guests are wine aficionados. There are a number of reasonably priced, delicious sparkling wines from California or Spain that would enliven your shower buffet.

PREPARATION TIMETABLE

Up to 1 month ahead:
* Make a list of all nonperishables (including food and beverages) and purchase them.
* Make Spicy Parmesan Palmiers; wrap airtight and freeze.
* Make Corn and Rosemary Madeleines; wrap airtight and freeze.

Up to 3 days ahead:
* Make vinaigrette for Couscous Salad; cover and refrigerate.

Up to 2 days ahead:
* Make Tropical Iced Tea Punch; cover and refrigerate.
* Make Fruit Ice Ring; cover with plastic wrap and freeze.
* Finish Couscous Salad; cover and refrigerate.
* Make dressing for Beet and Carrot Salad; cover and refrigerate.

15

* Make sauce for Chicken Breasts; cover and refrigerate.
* Make cake for Torta di Tiramisù; wrap tightly in plastic wrap and store at room temperature.
* Make syrup for Torta di Tiramisù; cover and store at room temperature.
* Set buffet table (without flowers).

Up to 1 day ahead:
* Finish Beet and Carrot Salad; cover and refrigerate.
* Make Chicken Breast rolls; cover and refrigerate.
* Finish Torta di Tiramisù; wrap loosely in plastic wrap and refrigerate.

Up to 8 hours ahead:
* Slice Chicken Breast rolls and place on a serving platter; cover and refrigerate.

Up to 2 hours ahead:
* Place sparkling wine or any other beverages that need to be chilled in ice-filled tubs.

Just before party:
* Fill punch bowl with Tropical Iced Tea Punch; unmold Fruit Ice Ring and place in bowl.
* Place flowers on buffet table.

Just before serving buffet:
* Transfer all food to bowls and platters; don't forget serving utensils.

About 1 hour before serving dessert:
* Make coffee; fill creamers and sugar bowls.

About 15 minutes before serving dessert:
* Remove torta from refrigerator.
* Boil water for tea; keep simmering on very low heat.

TROPICAL ICED TEA PUNCH WITH FRUIT ICE RING

Makes about 4 quarts, 14 to 20 servings

I always thought that the word *punch* came from the fact that most of these beverages pack a wallop. Research shows that the word comes from Sanskrit (*panch*), meaning "five," as the drink was originally concocted from five ingredients: lime, sugar, water, spices, and a fermented sap called *arrack*. A good punch must do double duty: it should be nonalcoholic and tasty enough for children, and be flavorful enough to spike, if desired. This punch fills these requirements. I serve a bottle of dark rum next to the punch so guests can indulge.

4 cups boiling water
1 cup superfine sugar (or granulated sugar processed until finely ground in a blender)
4 bags peach-flavored herbal tea
2 bags orange-pekoe tea
1 (46-ounce) can unsweetened pineapple juice
3 (12-ounce) cans mango or peach nectar
1½ cups lime juice
2 ripe mangoes, peeled, pitted, and cut into ¾-inch cubes (or use 2 cups fresh ripe peaches or thawed frozen peach slices)
1 (15-ounce) can crushed pineapple in heavy syrup
1 (750 ml) bottle of dark rum (optional)

1. In a large pitcher, combine boiling water, sugar, and tea bags. Stir to dissolve sugar, then let stand until tea is very strong and cooled, about 30 minutes. Strain into a large bowl, pressing hard on tea bags. Stir in pineapple, mango, and lime juices.

The punch can be prepared up to 2 days ahead, covered, and refrigerated.

2. Place mango cubes in a 4-cup ring mold. Add crushed pineapple with juice. Pour in enough punch to fill mold, about 1½ cups. Place in freezer and freeze until firm, at least overnight. *The ring mold can be prepared up to 2 days ahead and frozen.*

3. Pour remaining punch into a large punch bowl. Dip outside of ring mold in a large bowl of hot water until ice ring has melted enough to unmold, about 20 seconds. Unmold ring mold and place in punch bowl. Place ladle in bowl and serve punch cold, with a bottle of rum served on the side so each guest can add the liquor as desired.

SPICY PARMESAN PALMIERS

M a k e s   a b o u t   3   d o z e n

Sweet versions of these flaky pastries are often made in a much larger size and called "elephant ears" by American bakers. In France, they are called *palmiers*, as the shape is said to resemble a palm leaf. Although I can't really see the likeness myself, I agree that the French name is much more elegant and befitting a party. This variation is made zesty with a dash of cayenne, for a tasty hors d'oeuvre.

1 cup (4 ounces) freshly grated imported
   Parmesan cheese
¼ teaspoon ground hot red (cayenne)
   pepper
1 (17¼-ounce) package frozen puff pastry
   sheet, thawed

1. In a small bowl, combine cheese and red pepper. Carefully unfold 1 pastry sheet on a clean work surface. Sprinkle evenly with ¼ cup of cheese mixture. Using a rolling pin, press cheese into surface of pastry. Turn pastry over, sprinkle with another ¼ cup of cheese, and roll again. Tightly roll up each long side of pastry in a jelly-roll fashion until both sides meet in the center. Press sides together tightly to form a log. Tightly wrap pastry in plastic wrap and place on a baking sheet. Repeat with remaining pastry and cheese. Refrigerate until well chilled and firm, at least 2 hours. *The palmiers can be prepared up to this point 2 days ahead, or frozen for up to 2 weeks. If frozen, thaw overnight in the refrigerator before proceeding.*

2. Line 2 baking sheets with parchment paper or grease lightly. Unwrap pastry. Using a long, sharp, thin-bladed knife, cut into ½-inch-thick slices. Place palmiers 2 inches apart on prepared baking sheets. Cover with plastic wrap and refrigerate until chilled, at least 1 hour and up to 6 hours.

3. Position racks in center and top third of the oven and preheat to 400°F. Bake for 10 minutes. Turn and continue baking until crisp and golden brown, 8 to 10 minutes longer. Transfer to wire cake racks to cool slightly. Serve warm or at room temperature. *The baked palmiers can be prepared up to 2 days ahead, covered, and refrigerated. They can also be frozen for up to 1 month. Reheat without thawing in a 400°F. oven until crisp and heated through, about 5 minutes.*

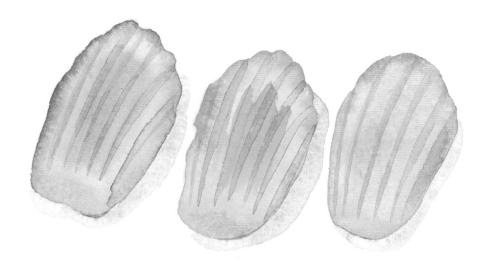

CORN AND ROSEMARY MADELEINES

Makes 2 dozen madeleines

In French literature, hot tea and madeleines are inseparable, thanks to the evocative prose of Marcel Proust in his novel, *Remembrance of Things Past,* where the main character's memory is triggered by the taste of the shell-shaped cakes dipped in hot tea. These madeleines, while still of shell shape, are not sweet at all, but rather made savory with cornmeal and rosemary. You will need madeleine molds to make the distinctive shapes, which are available at most kitchenware stores, but mini-muffin cups can also be used.

22

1 cup all-purpose flour
1 cup yellow cornmeal, preferably stone-
  ground
2 teaspoons baking powder
1 teaspoon dried rosemary
½ teaspoon salt
1 cup milk
2 large eggs
2 tablespoons unsalted butter, melted
Softened unsalted butter, for spreading
  (optional)

1. Position a rack in the top third of the oven and preheat to 400°F. Lightly butter and flour 24 madeleine molds (2 inches wide and 3¼ inches long each), tapping out any excess flour.

2. In a medium bowl, whisk together flour, cornmeal, baking powder, rosemary, and salt. In another bowl, whisk together milk, eggs, and melted butter until combined. Pour over dry ingredients and mix just until smooth. Do not overbeat. Spoon 1 tablespoon of batter into each prepared mold, and smooth the tops.

3. Bake until madeleines are golden brown and a toothpick inserted in center comes out clean, 15 to 18 minutes. Cool for 1 minute in pans. Use the tip of a knife to help remove madeleines from molds. Serve warm or at room temperature, with softened butter for spreading, if desired. *The madeleines can be prepared up to 1 day ahead, stored in plastic bags, and kept at room temperature. They can also be wrapped airtight and frozen for up to 1 month. If desired, reheat, wrapped in batches in aluminum foil, in a 350°F. oven until heated through, about 10 to 15 minutes.*

CHICKEN BREASTS STUFFED WITH HERBS AND CHEESE, WITH SWEET RED PEPPER SAUCE

Makes 12 servings

Chicken is always popular at large gatherings, and I have served this to thousands of guests at my catered events over the years. It can be made ahead in great numbers, and slicing the breasts allows you to get more servings than if you had served them whole. The sauce comes together like a dream. If you can't find soft goat cheese, you can use cream cheese.

8 (8 ounces each) chicken breasts, skin on but bones removed (see Note)
6 ounces rindless goat cheese (chèvre), such as Bucheron, at room temperature
½ cup fresh bread crumbs
1 garlic clove, crushed through a press

2 teaspoons chopped fresh chives, or 1 tablespoon chopped scallion
1 teaspoon chopped fresh rosemary leaves, or ½ teaspoon dried
1 teaspoon chopped fresh tarragon, or ½ teaspoon dried
¼ teaspoon freshly ground pepper
2 tablespoons olive oil
1 cup dry white wine
½ teaspoon salt

Sweet Red Pepper Sauce

3 large red bell peppers, seeded and cut into 1-inch pieces
¾ cup heavy cream
¾ cup chicken stock, preferably homemade, or use reduced-sodium canned broth
Salt and hot red pepper sauce to taste

1. Position a rack in top third of the oven and preheat to 350°F. Lightly oil a 10-by-15-inch baking pan.

2. Using a flat meat pounder or a rolling pin, pound each chicken breast between 2 sheets of moistened waxed paper to an even thickness of about ½ inch.

3. In a small bowl, combine softened cheese, bread crumbs, garlic, chives, rosemary, tarragon, and pepper. Divide cheese mixture evenly among breasts, placing in center. Fold in the short sides of breasts about 1 inch on each side, then roll up into thick cylinders, completely enclosing the cheese.

4. Place breasts in the prepared pan. Brush with oil, then pour wine over breasts. Season with salt and pepper. Bake, basting occasionally with

wine, until breasts are cooked through (a meat thermometer inserted into the center of a breast will read 165°F.), about 35 minutes. Cool completely. *The breasts can be prepared up to 1 day ahead, cooled, covered, and refrigerated.*

5. Meanwhile, make the sauce. In a medium saucepan, bring red peppers, cream, and stock to a simmer over medium heat. Cover and cook until peppers are tender, about 15 minutes. Uncover and increase the heat to high. Boil until liquid is reduced to about ½ cup, 10 to 15 minutes. Transfer to a food processor fitted with the metal blade (or in batches to a blender) and process until smooth. Season with salt and hot pepper sauce to taste. Transfer to a medium bowl and cool completely. Cover and refrigerate until chilled, at least 2 hours. *The sauce can*

be prepared up to 2 days ahead, cooled, covered, and refrigerated.

6. Using a sharp, thin-bladed knife, cut breasts diagonally into ¾-inch-thick slices. Arrange slices on a platter. *Roulades can be sliced and arranged up to 8 hours ahead. Cover platter tightly with plastic wrap and refrigerate.* Spoon a dollop of red pepper sauce on each breast and serve chilled.

Note: Buy 10- to 12-ounce chicken breast halves and ask the butcher to bone them, but leave the skin on. If the butcher won't cooperate, this task is easy to do at home. Using a sharp, thin-bladed knife, with the tip of the knife against the bones, scrape the meat away from the bones in 1 large piece. Save the bones to make into stock, if you wish. They can be wrapped airtight and frozen for up to 3 months.

COUSCOUS SALAD WITH SAFFRON VINAIGRETTE

Makes 12 to 16 servings

Couscous salad often becomes the object of conversation at my buffets—is it a pasta or a grain? Actually, it is a very tiny Moroccan pasta made from semolina flour. In North Africa it is steamed, but here it is most easily found in an "instant" boiled variety. Saffron, a costly spice consisting of the stigmas from small purple crocus, is an extravagant flavoring that befits a special occasion like a wedding celebration. However, many frugal cooks substitute an equal amount of turmeric to duplicate saffron's golden color.

Vinaigrette

⅓ cup lemon juice
1 garlic clove, crushed through a press
¾ teaspoon salt
½ teaspoon crumbled saffron threads
¼ teaspoon crushed hot red pepper flakes
1 cup olive oil

2½ cups water
2 tablespoons olive oil
1 (12-ounce) box quick-cooking couscous (about 1¾ cups)
3 medium zucchini, cut into ¼-inch dice
3 medium carrots, cut into ¼-inch dice
1 medium red bell pepper, seeded and cut into ¼-inch dice
1 cup raisins
⅓ cup chopped fresh parsley

1. Make the vinaigrette: In a medium bowl, whisk lemon juice, garlic, salt, saffron, and red pepper flakes. Gradually whisk in oil; set aside.

The vinaigrette can be prepared up to 3 days ahead, covered, and refrigerated.

2. In a medium saucepan, bring water and oil to a boil over high heat. Stir in couscous and return to a boil. Remove pan from heat, cover, and let stand for 5 minutes. Transfer to a large bowl, fluffing couscous with a fork.

3. In a large saucepan of boiling, lightly salted water, cook zucchini and carrots just until color is set,

about 1 minute. Drain, rinse under cold water, and drain again. Transfer to couscous. Add red pepper, raisins, and parsley and mix well. Add half the dressing and mix again. Cover and refrigerate until well chilled, at least 2 hours. *The salad can be prepared up to 2 days ahead, covered, and refrigerated.*

4. Just before serving, add remaining dressing and toss again. Serve cold or at room temperature.

BEET AND CARROT SALAD WITH WALNUT DRESSING

Makes 12 to 16 servings

I love grated fresh beets, and I live close to a farmer's market where I can get excellent ones year-round. They add such a gorgeous color to a buffet table that I devised a salad to feature their vibrant magenta. Placed side-by-side with ever-popular carrots, guests can choose to take a spoonful of either, or a little of both. A word of advice about this recipe: don't try to shred the vegetables without a food processor or a rotary hand grater. It's simply too much work to do by hand for this many people.

Walnut Dressing

½ cup raspberry vinegar (see Note)
½ cup minced shallots or scallions
4 teaspoons sugar
2 teaspoons salt
½ teaspoon freshly ground pepper
1½ cups French walnut or extra-virgin olive oil

2¼ pounds (weighed without greens) fresh beets (about 20 medium beets)
3 pounds (weighed without tops) fresh carrots (about 18 medium carrots)
1 cup finely chopped walnuts

1. Make the dressing: In a medium bowl, whisk vinegar, shallots, sugar, salt, and pepper until combined. Gradually whisk in oil. *The dressing can be made up to 2 days ahead, covered, and refrigerated.*

2. Trim and pare beets. Using a food

processor fitted with the shredding blade or a rotary hand grater, shred beets. You should have about 6 cups. Transfer to a large plastic bag.

3. Trim and peel carrots. Using a food processor fitted with the shredding blade or a rotary hand grater, shred carrots. You should have about 6 cups. Transfer to a large plastic bag.

4. Pour about ¾ cup of dressing into each bag of vegetables and toss well. Separately refrigerate salads and remaining dressing until well chilled, at least 2 hours. *The salads can be prepared up to 1 day ahead, stored in plastic bags, and refrigerated.*

5. Just before serving, divide remaining dressing and chopped walnuts between salads and toss separately. Taste and reseason with additional salt and pepper, if needed. Place sal-

ads in 2 separate mounds in a wide serving bowl. Serve immediately, with 2 separate spoons so guests can serve themselves.

Note: If raspberry vinegar is unavailable, delete the sugar and whisk 2 tablespoons seedless raspberry preserves into the vinegar mixture until completely dissolved.

TORTA DI TIRAMISÙ

Makes 12 servings

Tiramisù is the little dessert heard 'round the world. Originating in the Veneto region of Italy, it was nothing more than some leftover ladyfingers soaked in sweetened espresso, mixed with soft, rich mascarpone cheese, and served as a quick afternoon snack—in fact, it means "pick me up." I have started with the essential flavors and come up with a more sophisticated interpretation that can be displayed with pride on a crystal cake stand. I like to serve the cake with a fruit salad. Not only does the fruit complement the cake, but if some of your guests are dieting, they can have the salad for dessert and not feel too deprived.

There are two ingredients in this recipe that you may not be familiar with. Instant espresso powder is found at Italian grocers and many supermarkets. It is just the same as regular instant coffee, only a darker roast and stronger. You may use instant coffee instead, but it won't have the same punch or Italian authenticity. Another Italian ingredient, sweet Marsala, is found at liquor stores, and is simply sweeter than the regular "dry" Marsala. Sweet marsala is used in Italian baked goods, while the dry version should be saved for savory dishes, but can be substituted in this recipe if absolutely necessary. Increase the sugar in the espresso syrup to 1¼ cups if using dry Marsala.

Cake

1 cup cake flour (not self-rising)
¼ teaspoon salt
6 large eggs
1 cup granulated sugar
4 tablespoons unsalted butter, melted
1 teaspoon vanilla extract

Espresso Syrup

1 cup sugar
1 cup water
4 teaspoons instant espresso powder, or
   2 tablespoons instant coffee
¼ cup boiling water
½ cup sweet Marsala

2 cups mascarpone cheese
1¼ cups chilled heavy cream
3 tablespoons confectioners' sugar
1 ounce semisweet chocolate, grated on the
   large holes of a cheese grater
12 fresh rinsed, unhulled strawberries,
   for garnish

1. Make the cake: Position a rack in the center of the oven and preheat to 350°F. Lightly butter and flour a 10-inch springform pan. Line bottom of pan with a round of waxed paper. Sift flour and salt together through a wire sifter onto a piece of waxed paper.

2. In a large heatproof bowl, whisk eggs and sugar. Place bowl over a large saucepan of simmering water. Whisk constantly until eggs are warm to the touch and sugar is dissolved, about 2 minutes. Remove the bowl from the hot water. Using a handheld electric mixer set at high speed, beat the egg mixture until it is pale yellow and tripled in volume, about 5 minutes.

3. Sift about one-half of the flour mixture over the whipped eggs. Using a large balloon whisk or a

rubber spatula, gently fold in the flour mixture. Sift the remaining flour mixture over the batter and fold in. (Do this gently—don't worry if some flour remains visible.)

4. In a small bowl, combine the melted butter and vanilla. Transfer about 1 cup of the batter to the bowl and whisk until combined. Pour this mixture back into the batter and fold in just until combined and no flour is visible. Transfer to prepared pan and smooth the top.

5. Bake until top of cake springs back when pressed in center and shrinks away from sides of pan, about 30 minutes. Cool cake on a wire cake rack for 5 minutes. Invert onto rack and unmold. Peel off waxed paper. Turn right side up and cool completely. *The cake can be prepared up to 2 days ahead, cooled, wrapped*

tightly with plastic wrap, and stored at room temperature.

6. Make the espresso syrup: In a small saucepan, stir sugar and water over high heat until dissolved and boiling. Stop stirring and cook for 2 minutes. Remove from heat. In a small bowl, dissolve espresso powder in boiling water. Stir into syrup. Stir in Marsala. Cool completely. *The syrup can be prepared up to 2 days ahead, covered, and stored at room temperature.*

7. In a medium bowl, using a rubber spatula, mash and fold mascarpone cheese with ¼ cup heavy cream until smooth. In a chilled medium bowl, using a handheld mixer set at high speed, beat heavy cream with confectioners' sugar until soft peaks form. Fold whipped cream into cheese mixture until combined.

8. Using a long serrated knife, trim "skin" off top of cake. Slice cake horizontally into 2 even layers. Place one layer on the bottom of the 10-inch springform pan. Using a large pastry brush, drizzle and brush cake with about half the espresso syrup. Spread with one-third of cheese mixture. Top with second cake layer, and drizzle and brush with remaining syrup. Using a metal spatula, frost the top and sides of the cake with the remaining cheese mixture. Sprinkle the top of the cake with the grated chocolate. Place the strawberries around the outside edge of the cake.

9. Insert a few wooden toothpicks around cake surface and wrap cake with plastic wrap (the toothpicks will keep the wrap from touching the icing). Refrigerate at least 6 hours or overnight. *The cake can be prepared up to 1 day, covered, and refrigerated.*

A CELEBRATION TEA

A Selection of Fine Teas
Milk or Cream, Demerara Sugar, Lemon Slices

SAVORIES
PARMESAN-PROSCIUTTO SCONES
ROQUEFORT AND WALNUT TRIANGLES
POTTED SHRIMP AND WATERCRESS SANDWICHES
CUCUMBER SANDWICHES WITH SMOKED SALMON BUTTER
SMOKED TURKEY AND APRICOT SALAD TARTLETS

SWEETS
CARROT-CURRANT TEA LOAVES
DRAMBUIE-SOAKED GINGERBREAD
VICTORIA'S JAM ROULADE

For 8 to 12 people

A TEA PARTY IS A fun way to share the afternoon with friends and enjoy a flavorful variety of sweet and savory nibbles. And it's a superior way to celebrate the upcoming birth of a new baby. Dispel the notion that a tea is a stuffy, boring affair served by starched, ancient retainers, or that you must hold your pinky up while you sip. And tea has become a very popular beverage in the last few years. Before, people may have been familiar with only the supermarket variety, but tastes in tea have become much broader and sophisticated. A tea party gives the chance to brew a few different blends and have a tasting, allowing the guests to discover new favorites.

The perfect time for a baby shower tea is on a weekend afternoon about 1 P.M. In Britain, and at fine American hotels, the proper time for a high tea is between 4 and 6 P.M., as it is considered a heavy snack between lunch and dinner, or even as an early supper. However, at home, why not serve this versatile and special mini-meal whenever it suits you? The menu must include both sweet and savory items. Where appropriate, the items are cut into individual portions to eat as finger food. Many of the guests will be using the tea as a substitute for lunch, so there has to be enough food to fill them up. However, others will be looking at the tea as a snack, so the food should be light. The solution is to offer a large selection of teatime goodies, so everyone can pick and choose as desired. While the visual appeal of food is always important, it is even more so at a tea, where the viands are traditionally cut into bite-size shapes. In each recipe, I specify what tools and utensils will help you create beautiful tea sandwiches, canapés, hors d'oeuvres, and sweets that a Ritz would be proud of.

The cultivation and culture of tea is complex, but all you really need to know is that there are three varieties with distinct flavors: green, black, and oolong. I like to serve one of each, perhaps a Gunpowder, an English Breakfast blend, and a Formosa Oolong. Because the quality of your tea will establish the mood for the entire affair, buy the best. Go to your local coffee and tea store or a specialty grocer to make your selection, not the supermarket. With the recent proliferation of coffee and tea merchants, excellent tea is easy to find. Reliable mail order sources include Starbucks (1-800-872-7282), Peet's (1-800-999-2132), and McNulty's (1-212-242-5351.)

I rent a large samovar to keep water piping hot, and prepare separate pots of tea as needed, using loose tea. You can put out a variety of tea bags, allowing the guests to make tea directly in their cups, but brewing loose tea is the preferred method and gives the best flavor. If you have a gorgeous antique tea service, you will probably choose to make just one kind

of tea (unless you have more than one antique tea server!).

If you are making a pot of tea, the procedure is simplicity itself. Use freshly drawn, cold water that has been just boiled (or if you are using a samovar, fill it with boiled water and keep it piping hot with its heater or flame). Allow about 6 ounces of water per cup. Preheat the pot by filling with very hot tap water and letting it stand for a few minutes. Empty out the pot and add 1 heaping teaspoon of loose tea (or 1 tea bag) per person, plus one extra spoon for the pot, then fill with the boiling water. If you are using a tea bag, check the box, as some brands recommend one tea bag for 12 ounces of water, or 2 cups. Stir once, cover, and let steep for at least 3 minutes and up to 5 min-

41

utes. If using loose tea, place a tea strainer into each cup before pouring the tea. Tea cozies are handy to keep the pots warm between pourings.

You need to serve only three things to flavor the tea—milk or light cream (half-and-half), sugar, and lemon slices. The milk should not be ice cold; it can be warmed briefly in a microwave oven to take off the chill. I like to serve demerara sugar—beige sugar crystals available at specialty grocers—which is more flavorful than refined white sugar. If you can't find demerara sugar, serve sugar cubes for that touch of elegance. The lemon should be sliced into thin rounds and placed on a plate. If you have the patience, pick out the seeds with the tip of a knife.

All of the foods in this menu are easy to make ahead, and can be served at room temperature. If you wish, however, reheat the baked goods in batches and serve them warm. The sandwiches are best served chilled, so put out only as many as will be served within a half-hour's time, then replace as needed. The sweets can be served at the same time. It may be best to serve the food on a dining-room table or sideboard buffet-style, with the tea service set up in the conversation area of the room on a coffee table. Set the buffet with the appropriate plates, forks, and napkins, and place the tea server, tea, teapots (if using), teacups, and saucers with strainers, teaspoons, milk, sugar, and lemon on the tea table. One wants to have the tea near the center of conversation, as it is usually the host or hostess's duty to serve the tea to each guest (asking, of course, what the guest prefers in the way of milk, sugar, or lemon). You don't want to go into another room to do this.

For the finishing touch, place a small arrangement of flowers, even a simple nosegay, on the tea table. Let it be colorful but restrained, as the tea service should take center stage in all its highly polished glory. In spring and summer, pick blossoms from the garden to decorate the platters. However, use nontoxic edible flowers, such as roses, violets, Johnny-jump-ups, and nasturtiums, and make certain they have not been sprayed by chemicals. If you have any doubts about the flowers, don't use them as a garnish, but keep them safely in a vase for all to admire.

PREPARATION TIMETABLE

Up to 1 month ahead:
* Make tartlet shells for Smoked Turkey and Apricot Salad; wrap airtight and freeze.
* Make Carrot-Currant Tea Loaves; wrap airtight and freeze.

Up to 2 weeks ahead:
* Make Parmesan-Prosciutto Scones; wrap airtight and freeze.

* Make Roquefort and Walnut Triangles; wrap airtight and freeze.

Up to 5 days ahead:
* Make Drambuie-Soaked Gingerbread; wrap tightly in plastic wrap and store at room temperature.
* Polish all silver utensils.

Up to 2 days ahead:
* Make Smoked Turkey and Apricot Salad, cover, and refrigerate.

* Make cake for Victoria's Jam Roulade; wrap tightly in plastic wrap and store at room temperature.

Up to 1 day ahead:
* Partially set table (without flowers); place cups, spoons, and forks upside down to discourage collecting dust.
* Make Potted Shrimp spread; cover and refrigerate.
* Wash and stem watercress for Potted Shrimp and Watercress Sandwiches; wrap in paper towels, then store in a plastic bag and refrigerate.
* Make Smoked Salmon Butter; cover and refrigerate.
* Fill and frost Victoria's Jam Roulade; cover in plastic wrap and refrigerate.

Up to 8 hours ahead:
* Bring Potted Shrimp Spread to room temperature; make Potted Shrimp and Watercress Sandwiches; cover and refrigerate.
* Bring Smoked Salmon Butter to room temperature; make Cucumber Sandwiches with Smoked Salmon Butter.
* Fill tartlets with Smoked Turkey and Apricot Salad; cover with plastic wrap and refrigerate.
* Thinly slice Carrot-Currant Tea Loaves; cover and store at room temperature.
* Fill creamer, sugar bowl, and slice lemons.

Up to 30 minutes ahead:
* Boil water for samovar, if using, and fill samovar.
* Bake frozen Roquefort and Walnut Triangles.

Just before guest's arrival:
* Place food on platters and set on buffet table.

PARMESAN-PROSCIUTTO SCONES

Makes about 20 scones

In Britain, scones are as much a part of the tea ritual as hot water. Originally, they were cut into triangles and cooked on griddles, but nowadays they are more likely to be round and baked. (If you have them, use heart-shaped biscuit cutters for an even nicer effect.) Savory flavorings, such as the cheese and ham featured here, are recent developments in scone history. My recipe, perfected after years of catering high teas, guarantees the lightest scones ever.

1½ cups cake flour (not self-rising)
1½ cups all-purpose flour
1 tablespoon cream of tartar
1½ teaspoons baking soda
¼ teaspoon salt
¼ teaspoon freshly ground pepper
12 tablespoons (1½ sticks) unsalted butter, chilled, cut into ½-inch pieces
½ cup (4 ounces) finely chopped prosciutto
½ cup (4 ounces) freshly grated imported Parmesan cheese
1¼ cups plus 2 tablespoons buttermilk
Buttermilk, for brushing
Softened unsalted butter, for spreading (optional)

1. Position racks in the top third and center of the oven and preheat to 400°F.

2. Sift cake and all-purpose flours, cream of tartar, baking soda, salt, and pepper into a medium bowl. Using a pastry blender or 2 knives, cut

butter into flour until mixture resembles coarse meal. Stir in prosciutto and cheese. Add buttermilk and stir until dough is moistened and begins to hold together. Using floured hands, knead briefly in the bowl just to form a soft dough. (Light handling is the secret to tender scones.)

3. Turn dough out onto a lightly floured work surface. Pat out to ½ inch thickness. Using a 2½-inch round or heart-shaped biscuit cutter, cut out scones and place 1 inch apart on ungreased baking sheets. Brush tops of scones lightly with additional buttermilk.

4. Bake until well risen and golden brown, 15 to 20 minutes. Halfway through baking, change positions of baking sheets from top to bottom. Serve warm or at room temperature, with softened butter for spreading, if desired. *The scones can be prepared up to 1 day ahead, cooled, and stored in plastic bags at room temperature. Or freeze in airtight containers for up to 2 weeks. Defrost before reheating. Reheat, if desired, loosely wrapped in aluminum foil, in a 350°F. oven until heated through, about 10 minutes.*

ROQUEFORT AND WALNUT TRIANGLES

Makes 3 2 triangles

These small triangle-shaped morsels are filled with a robust combination of Roquefort cheese, walnuts, and port wine.

6 ounces Roquefort cheese, or other blue cheese, softened
2 ounces cream cheese, softened
⅓ cup finely chopped walnuts
3 tablespoons dried bread crumbs
2 tablespoons port wine, such as tawny (or use heavy cream)
⅛ teaspoon freshly ground pepper
8 sheets (about 12-by-17-inches) thawed filo dough
6 tablespoons unsalted butter, melted

1. Position the racks in the top third and center of the oven and preheat to 350°F. Lightly butter a large baking sheet.

2. In a medium bowl, mash together the Roquefort and cream cheeses. Stir in walnuts, bread crumbs, wine, and pepper.

3. Place a filo sheet on a work surface, short side facing you. Cover remaining sheets with plastic wrap and a dampened kitchen towel to keep from drying out. Brush filo sheet well with some melted butter. Using a sharp knife and a ruler, cut lengthwise into 4 strips, about 3 inches wide. Place a rounded teaspoon of the filling at the end of a strip, off to one corner. Fold the opposing corner of filo over to opposite edge, covering the filling, and continue folding the strip as you would a flag, keeping a triangular shape with each fold. Place on prepared baking sheet and cover with plastic wrap. Continue procedure with melted butter, filo, and fill-

ing. *The triangles can be prepared up to 2 weeks ahead and frozen. Place in aluminum foil trays, separating the layers with plastic wrap. Overwrap tightly with plastic wrap, and then aluminum foil. Do not defrost before baking.*

4. Brush tops of triangles with remaining butter. Bake until golden brown, changing the positions of the baking sheets from top to bottom halfway through baking, about 15 minutes. If frozen, bake for 5 to 10 minutes longer. Let cool for 10 minutes before serving. *The baked tri-*

angles can be prepared up to 8 hours ahead and stored at room temperature. Reheat, loosely covered with aluminum foil, in a 350°F. oven until heated through, about 10 minutes.

Note: Frozen filo dough makes flaky, golden brown baked goods, but it can be a little tricky to work with. Defrost it slowly overnight in the refrigerator, and while forming your pastries, keep the remaining dough covered with plastic wrap and a damp cloth, or it will dry out.

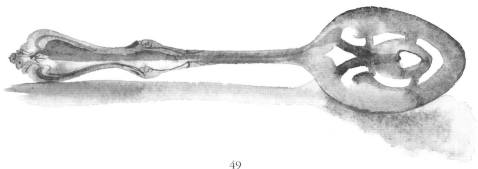

POTTED SHRIMP AND WATERCRESS SANDWICHES

Makes 60 small triangular sandwiches

These are one of my most popular tea sandwiches, with a delicate shrimp spread perked up by peppery watercress leaves.

Potted Shrimp Spread

8 ounces medium shrimp
8 ounces cream cheese, at room temperature
1 tablespoon chopped fresh dill
2 teaspoons lime juice
¼ teaspoon Worcestershire sauce
Hot pepper sauce, such as Tabasco, to taste

30 slices (about 1 pound, 12 ounces) firm white bread (see Note)
1 cup watercress leaves, rinsed, thick stems removed

1. Make the potted shrimp spread: Bring a medium saucepan of lightly salted water to a boil over high heat. Add shrimp and cook until firm and pink, 2 to 3 minutes. Drain and rinse under cold running water. Peel and devein shrimp.

2. In a food processor fitted with the metal blade, pulse shrimp until chopped. Add cream cheese, dill, lime juice, Worcestershire, and hot pepper sauce and process until smooth. Transfer to a small bowl. You may also use a large knife to mince shrimp, then combine in a bowl with remaining ingredients, mashing until smooth. *The spread can be prepared up to 1 day ahead, covered, and refrigerated. Let stand at room temperature until spreadable, about 1 hour, before proceeding.*

3. Using a long, thin-bladed sharp knife, trim crusts from bread to form each slice of bread into a 3-inch square. (Stack bread slices 2 or 3 slices at a time to trim.) Spread about 1 tablespoon of spread onto 15 bread squares. Top with watercress leaves. Top each with one of the remaining 15 bread squares to make 15 sandwiches. Cut diagonally into 4 triangular sandwiches. *The sandwiches are best prepared as close to serving time as possible, but can be prepared up to 8 hours ahead. Arrange the sandwiches on a baking sheet, separating the layers with plastic wrap. Wrap the entire sheet tightly in plastic wrap and refrigerate until ready to serve.* Serve chilled.

Note: The choice of bread is very important. It should be firm, with a close crumb, and with a flat, not domed, top. Pepperidge Farm is an excellent supermarket brand, but your local bakery may be able to supply the proper type, as well. For whole wheat bread, you may have to go to a natural foods store. If the bread is domed, simply trim the dome off.

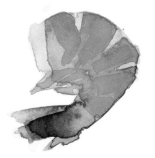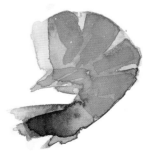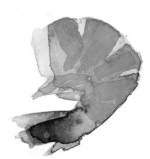

CUCUMBER SANDWICHES WITH SMOKED SALMON BUTTER

M a k e s   4 0   (2 ¼ - i n c h)
r o u n d   s a n d w i c h e s

Cucumber sandwiches are "must-haves" at a proper tea. This open-faced version is quite attractive, and the smoked salmon butter "moisture-proofs" the bread from the cucumbers. For cutting the bread slices into neat rounds, use a 2¼-inch round biscuit cutter. To cut the cucumbers into thin slices without aggravation, use a mandoline, a very worthwhile investment. This slicing tool is available at kitchenware shops in an inexpensive Swiss version. (The professional French-made models are very expensive.)

Smoked Salmon Butter

4 ounces smoked salmon
8 tablespoons (1 stick) unsalted butter, at room temperature
⅛ teaspoon freshly ground pepper

20 slices (about 1½ pounds) firm whole wheat bread (see Note, page 51)
1 small seedless (English) cucumber, cut into 40 (⅛-inch-thick) slices
2 tablespoons chopped fresh chives

1. Make the smoked salmon butter: In a food processor fitted with the metal blade, process smoked salmon until finely chopped. Add butter and pepper and process until smooth. Transfer to a small bowl. *The butter can be prepared up to 2 days ahead, covered, and refrigerated. Let stand at room temperature until spreadable, about 1 hour, before proceeding.*

2. Using a 2¼-inch round biscuit cutter, cut 2 rounds out of each slice of bread. Spread about 1 teaspoon of salmon butter over each bread round. Top each with a cucumber slice and sprinkle with chives. *The sandwich es can be made up to 8 hours ahead. Arrange the sandwiches on a baking sheet, separating the layers with plastic wrap. Press plastic wrap directly on the surface of the top layer. Refrigerate until ready to serve.* Serve chilled.

SMOKED TURKEY AND APRICOT SALAD TARTLETS

Makes about 3 ½ dozen tartlets

Mini-tartlets are always a labor of love, but I offer a foolproof pastry that results in a crisp yet tender shell that holds up so well to the moist salad that you can fill the tartlets hours ahead and not worry about their getting soggy. And remember, the shells can be made weeks ahead and frozen. Old tartlet recipes call for European molds, but I prefer to use easy-to-find mini-muffin cups. If you have the old molds, you can use them, but you may use twice as much dough per shell, and the yield will be different. The salad is an artful blending of many flavors and textures—smoky turkey, sweet apricots, crunchy celery, and tangy mustard.

Cream Cheese Tartlets

8 tablespoons (1 stick) unsalted butter,
at room temperature
1 (3-ounce) package cream cheese, at room
temperature
1 cup all-purpose flour
¼ teaspoon salt

Smoked Turkey Salad

6 ounces smoked turkey, cut into ¼-inch
dice
3 ounces dried apricots, cut into ¼-inch dice
(about ⅓ cup)
1 small celery rib, cut into ¼-inch dice
(about ⅓ cup)
2 tablespoons mayonnaise
1 tablespoon sour cream
1 tablespoon honey mustard
½ teaspoon dried tarragon
⅛ teaspoon salt
⅛ teaspoon freshly ground pepper

2 tablespoons chopped fresh parsley, for
garnish

1. Make the cream cheese tartlets:
Position a rack in top third and center of the oven and preheat to 375°F.
In a medium bowl, using a handheld electric mixer set at medium speed, beat butter and cream cheese until smooth. Using a wooden spoon, stir in flour and salt to make a soft dough. Gather into a thick disc, wrap in waxed paper, and refrigerate for 30 minutes.

2. Using a heaping teaspoon of dough for each tartlet, press dough firmly and evenly into 42 ungreased mini-muffin tins (1¼ inches wide and 1 inch deep). Prick dough well with a fork. Refrigerate until firm, about 10 minutes.

3. Bake shells until the crusts are lightly browned, 10 to 15 minutes. Halfway during baking, change positions of tins from top to bottom. Using the tip of a small knife, lift out the crusts and cool completely on a wire rack. *The tartlet crusts can be prepared up to 1 day ahead, stored in an airtight container at room temperature. They can also be frozen, wrapped airtight, for up to 1 month.*

4. Make the smoked turkey salad: In a small bowl, combine all ingredients. *The salad can be prepared up to 2 days ahead, covered, and refrigerated.*

5. Fill tartlet shells with salad and sprinkle with the parsley. *The tartlets can be filled up to 8 hours ahead, covered, and refrigerated.* Serve chilled or at room temperature.

CARROT-CURRANT TEA LOAVES

Makes two 8-by-4-inch loaves

Not too sweet, studded with walnuts and sherry-imbibed currants, this quick bread is right at home on a tea cart. A type of cake called a "cut and butter" loaf, the name refers to the very British fashion of having each slice lightly buttered. I find it hard to resist decorating the carrot cake slices in a more American fashion, with a rosette of cream cheese.

1 cup dried currants
¼ cup Oloroso or cream sherry or apple juice
3 cups all-purpose flour
2 teaspoons ground cinnamon
1½ teaspoons baking soda
1¼ teaspoons salt
1 teaspoon baking powder
2 cups sugar
1 cup vegetable oil
3 large eggs, at room temperature
1 teaspoon vanilla extract
2 cups shredded carrots (from about 6 medium carrots)
1 cup coarsely chopped walnuts
2 ounces cream cheese, softened (optional)

1. In a small bowl, combine currants and sherry. Let stand for 1 hour, stirring occasionally. Strain over a bowl, reserving sherry and soaked currants.

2. Position a rack in the center of the oven and preheat to 350°F. Butter

and flour two 8-by-4-inch loaf pans, tapping out excess flour. Line bottom of pans with waxed paper. Sift together flour, cinnamon, baking soda, salt, and baking powder through a wire sieve onto a piece of waxed paper.

3. In a large bowl, using a handheld electric mixer set at high speed, beat sugar and oil until combined, about 1 minute. One at a time, beat in eggs, beating well after each addition. Beat in reserved sherry and vanilla. With a wooden spoon, beat in carrots. Gradually stir in flour mixture. (The batter will be stiff.) Stir in currants and walnuts. Transfer to prepared loaf pans and smooth tops.

4. Bake until a toothpick inserted in center of loaves comes out clean, about 1 hour. Cool for 10 minutes on a wire cake rack. Invert onto racks

and remove pans. Carefully peel off waxed paper. Place right side up and cool completely. *The loaves can be prepared up to 3 days ahead, wrapped tightly in plastic wrap and stored at room temperature, or frozen for up to 1 month.*

5. Slice thinly before serving. If desired, place cream cheese in a pastry bag fitted with a large star-tipped pastry tube, such as Ateco number 5. Just before serving, pipe a rosette onto each slice.

DRAMBUIE-SOAKED GINGERBREAD

Makes 12 to 16 servings

Most people tend to think of gingerbread as a holiday dessert, but this is so good I serve it year-round. (This is not to say that I neglect it

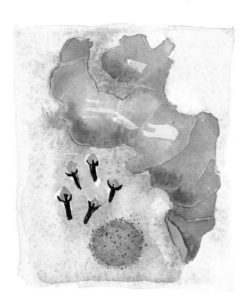

Gingerbread

2¼ cups all-purpose flour
2 teaspoons ground ginger
2 teaspoons ground cinnamon
2 teaspoons baking soda
½ teaspoon ground cloves
½ teaspoon salt
1 cup (2 sticks) unsalted butter, at room
    temperature
1 cup packed light brown sugar
2 large eggs, at room temperature
1 cup unsulphured molasses
¼ cup Drambuie
¾ cup hot water

4 tablespoons (½ stick) unsalted butter,
    melted
⅓ cup Drambuie
Confectioners' sugar, for dusting
Sweetened whipped cream, for serving
    (optional)

at Christmas—in fact, this recipe is one of my favorite foods to make and give.) While I prefer Scotch-based Drambuie, you may experiment with other liqueurs such as Southern Comfort or Grand Marnier, but do not delete the liqueur totally. Offer teetotalers a slice of Victoria's Jam Roulade.

1. Position a rack in center of oven and preheat to 350°F. Butter and

flour the inside of a 10-inch fluted tube pan. Sift together flour, ginger, cinnamon, baking soda, cloves, and salt onto a large piece of waxed paper; set aside.

2. In a large bowl, using a handheld electric mixer set at high speed, beat butter and brown sugar until very light in color, about 2 minutes. One at a time, beat in eggs. Beat in molasses and ¼ cup Drambuie.

3. Reduce mixer speed to low. In 3 additions, beat in dry ingredients, scraping down sides of bowl with a rubber spatula as needed. Beat in hot water. Transfer to prepared pan and smooth top.

4. Bake until a toothpick inserted in center of cake comes out clean, 50 minutes to 1 hour. Cool cake in pan on wire cake rack for 10 minutes.

5. In a small bowl, whisk melted butter and ⅓ cup Drambuie. Using a large pastry brush, drizzle and brush half of the glaze over top of warm cake in pan. (Do this gradually so glaze soaks into cake.) Let stand for 20 minutes. Invert cake onto wire cake rack and remove pan. Brush cake with remaining glaze. Cool completely. *The cake can be prepared up to 5 days ahead, cooled, wrapped tightly in plastic wrap, and stored at room temperature.*

6. Place cake on a serving platter and sift confectioners' sugar over top before serving with optional whipped cream.

VICTORIA'S JAM ROULADE

Makes 12 servings

One of the most popular sweets on a British tea cart is Victoria Cake—sponge cake layers filled with jam and slathered with whipped cream, reportedly a favorite of the former queen's. I like to turn the cake into a jelly roll, which makes for a more interesting presentation and increases the number of servings.

Cake Roulade

¾ cup cake flour (not self-rising)
1 teaspoon baking powder
¼ teaspoon salt
4 large eggs, separated, at room temperature
¾ cup granulated sugar, divided
¾ teaspoon vanilla extract
⅛ teaspoon cream of tartar
Confectioners' sugar, for sifting

1⅓ cups blackberry preserves
1½ cups heavy (whipping) cream, chilled
2 tablespoons confectioners' sugar
½ teaspoon vanilla extract
Fresh edible flowers (see page 43) or candied violets, for garnish (optional)

1. Make the cake roulade: Position a rack in the center of the oven and preheat to 350°F. Lightly butter and flour sides of a 10-by-15-by-1-inch jelly-roll pan. Line bottom of pan with waxed paper. Sift the flour, baking powder, and salt through a wire sieve onto a large piece of waxed paper.

2. In a large bowl, using a handheld electric mixer set at high speed, beat egg yolks and 6 tablespoons of sugar until thick and pale yellow, about 3 minutes. Beat in vanilla.

3. In another large bowl, using clean, dry beaters, beat egg whites at low speed until foamy. Add cream of tartar, increase speed to medium-high, and beat until soft peaks form. Still beating, gradually add remaining 6 tablespoons sugar until stiff, shiny peaks form. Stir about one-fourth of egg whites into yolk mixture to lighten it. Pour remaining whites over lightened yolk mixture, then sift in half of the flour mixture. Using a rubber spatula or large balloon whisk, fold together gently (a few traces of flour should remain). Sift in remaining flour and fold until batter is blended. Transfer to prepared pan and smooth with a metal spatula, especially in the corners.

4. Bake until cake springs back when pressed in the center with a finger, about 15 minutes.

5. Meanwhile, sift confectioners' sugar evenly over a clean kitchen towel. Invert cake onto sugar-coated towel. Carefully peel off waxed paper. Place waxed paper back on top of cake. Starting at a long end, using the towel as an aid, roll up cake into a spiral and wrap in towel. Cool completely, seam side down, on a wire cake rack. *The cake can be prepared up to 1 day ahead. Cool completely, then remove the towel, but not the waxed paper. Keeping the cake rolled, wrap tightly in plastic wrap. Store at room temperature.*

6. When cake is cool, unroll cake and discard waxed paper. Spread evenly with preserves, and reroll cake. Transfer to an oblong serving platter.

7. In a chilled, medium bowl, using a handheld electric mixer set at medium speed, beat cream, 2 tablespoons confectioners' sugar, and vanilla just until stiff peaks form. Do not overbeat or the cream may separate. Transfer about 1½ cups of whipped cream to a pastry bag fitted with a large star tube, such as Ateco number 5. Spread cake evenly with whipped cream. Using the pastry bag, decorate the roulade with rosettes and swirls. To wrap roulade in plastic wrap without the wrap marring the whipped cream frosting, insert several toothpicks in roulade, allowing them to protrude 1 inch from the surface, then cover loosely but completely with plastic wrap. Refrigerate until ready to serve. *The finished cake can be prepared up to 1 day ahead, covered, and refrigerated.*

8. When ready to serve, unwrap roulade and remove toothpicks, smoothing over holes with the tip of a spatula. Decorate the cake with edible flowers or the candied violets, if using. Serve chilled, using a serrated knife to cut crosswise into slices.